YOU WERE
BORN TO
FLY

Be Original,
Be the Best
YOU

DANIEL GOMEZ

www.selfpublishn30day

Published by *Self Publish -N- 30 Days*

Copyright 2018 Daniel Gomez Enterprises, LLC.

Printed in the United States of America

ISBN: 978-1725824669

1. Inspiration 2. Leadership

Daniel Gomez: Daniel Gomez Enterprises, LLC.

You Were Born To Fly

Disclaimer/Warning:

This book is dedicated to my wife, Mari,
and to my children, Alicia, Julian, and Brittany.
You inspire me and fill my heart with love
and joy every day.

CONTENTS

Introduction

Conclusion

INTRODUCTION

Of course, a person cannot physically fly, but with technology, we have come as close to it as possible with being transported by way of an airplane. I often see birds and just imagine how carefree they are. I relate the similarities with birds soaring in the sky to people skydiving.

While I have never experienced skydiving, I could only imagine the adrenaline and weightlessness associated with jumping aimlessly out of an airplane. They are falling through the sky with absolutely NO CONTROL. I have often wondered what someone's thoughts were seconds before they JUMPED.

Once they are already falling, why waste the experience thinking about what can go wrong instead of enjoying it? While you have time in this world, there's no reason to waste time thinking negatively instead of seeing the positive. The only thing that gives skydivers hope is the parachute. The parachute is what keeps them from being injured; it's their HOPE. What if I told you everything that is in you is within the confines of the parachute, but you are going to have to FLY before you can RELEASE it?

Your beliefs, persistence, imagination and EVERYTHING you possess for success is within reach.

Every moment you are breathing is a moment closer to death OR every second you live, you can adapt a positive outlook on your life and be much happier as a result. Your perception is your reality. How do you see your life?

I have no doubt that many of you want to live a life filled with happiness, joy, and prosperity. A life that every individual would love to have. Perhaps you want to FLY, but don't know which direction to go! The only thing holding you back is the how.

How do you obtain a fulfilling life?

How do you overcome situations to excel?

How do you know what you need to do?

I plan to answer all of these questions and more! My desire is to help you develop a positive attitude, seek confidence, pay more attention to your thinking, and become more in touch with your definite purpose in life.

The unhappiness many of us experience is because we are not living the lives we were created to live. You were created for a purpose. You have a destiny to fulfill.

My contribution to your success in life is this book. *You Were Born to Fly* will assist you in developing the life skills you need to live a prosperous and abundant life. It will help you learn how to grow and develop yourself. To become the person you were created to be. God did not create you to be mediocre; He created you to live a life of abundance.

I believe we all have potential inside of us that is dying to come out. Everyone is equipped with the potential to be great, potential to accomplish amazing feats in this world, potential to have amazing relationships with loved ones, and the potential to have the career we desire. Tap into it every day of your life. You are worth it. You have dreams on the inside wanting to come out. Don't be scared to act on your thoughts and ideas. Are you ready to live your life to the fullest?

My recommendation to you, read each chapter twice to allow it to sink into your subconscious mind. Read this book as if you are going to teach it; it will help you retain more of what you read.

After you've completed reading for the second time, write down what really stood out to you. Application is essential. If you can take away two great ideas that will change and improve the quality of your life, then my mission in writing this book was a success.

I want to encourage you to always believe in yourself and in your abilities. Never give up on your life! You are stronger than you believe. You are capable of accomplishing more than you believe you can. Continue investing in your life.

You cannot change your life until you change your thinking and your daily habits. Challenge yourself to learn and grow every day, it will take you places you could never imagine. Why walk through life discouraged when *You Were Born to Fly?*

CHAPTER 1

CONFIDENCE

Confidence is a mindset; it can either make you or break you in life. Confident people inspire others and give them a sense of boldness that surges into every sector of their lives. They inspire confidence in their friends, employees, and family. You might be asking yourself, what is confidence? It is described as a belief in one's self and one's ability to succeed.

You can spot a person with confidence from miles away. When a person has confidence, you can see it in their eyes. You can see it in the way they walk and the way they talk. You see it in the way they carry themselves daily. They radiate positivity and live a solution oriented lifestyle. Confidence gives you the ability to discover the gifts and talents you have.

When I think of a person with confidence, I think of Mr. Henry Finley. Mr. Finley is the GM at McCombs Ford West, a dealership in San Antonio, Texas.

I had the pleasure of meeting and working with Mr. Finley recently. From the very first day I met him, he exuberantly expressed confidence and it was contagious! He had such an undefeated mindset, that he and his staff could accomplish any feat that was set before them.

When a leader has confidence in himself it trickles down to his employees, like a domino effect which allows them to start believing in themselves.

As we sat in his office one day, discussing our game plan for the month, I remember a couple of his employees coming into his office to discuss a matter at hand. I recall the employees not being too sure of themselves, you could tell by the way they interacted in the conversation and their body language. The body language of a person tells you everything. If a person has their head down or is fidgeting, this could be a sign that they are lacking tenacity and appear hopeless.

I loved the way Mr. Finley responded. You could feel his confidence being transferred to his employees. I observed as his employees' body language transformed before my eyes. They stood up straight, with their shoulders abroad and their countenances transformed from exasperation to excitement.

Mr. Finley reassured them that everything was going to be all right. He explained to them that there wasn't an issue or problem that was too big that could not be resolved to the customer's satisfaction. Now while this confidence gave the customer satisfaction, having confidence in your life will create personal satisfaction as well. Often times, people that live with uncertainty never experience fulfillment.

Thankfully, Mr. Finley took the time to coach and mentor his employees in a way that not only resolved the issue, but helped develop and build his employees' confidence. Their entire demeanor had changed.

Sometimes in life, people just need some reassurance that everything is going to be okay. We all have some level of confidence within us, we just need to be reminded of it at times. When you have a leader like Mr. Finley that brings out the best in people, it helps you to believe in yourself, believe in your abilities, and gives reassurance that all things are possible.

That is what a leader with confidence can do for an organization; he raises the level of self-confidence in the entire organization. It's amazing how the power one person has inside of them has the ability to affect and build the confidence level of everyone they interact with.

There is unlimited possibility inside every one of us. I believe, if more leaders led like Mr. Henry Finley, many organizations would develop and grow to reach milestones they never thought possible.

I want you to consider this thought, if you are a business owner, maybe your employee has never been instilled with confidence. They may have never had a supervisor who believed in them and their abilities. The probability of their last employer taking the time to coach and guide them and build their self-confidence is probably zero to none. The probability

> SOMETIMES IN LIFE, PEOPLE JUST NEED SOME REASSURANCE THAT EVERYTHING IS GOING TO BE OKAY.

of their friends instilling confidence in them is most likely zero to none.

The probability of their parents building up their self-esteem and telling them they can go out and conquer the world, to accomplish whatever they want to in life, is probably nonexistent.

You see, most people haven't been instilled with a confident mindset in their childhood, employment, or their relationships. They've been taught to play it safe. No one may have told them to venture out into the world and believe in themselves the way that they should.

Most people were instructed from their youth to find a decent job, work hard and eventually you will move up the corporate ladder. People are trained with the mindset to be average.

> PEOPLE ARE TRAINED WITH THE MINDSET TO BE AVERAGE.

Instead of being built up to be a powerhouse, being trained with the mindset that you can achieve anything you want to in life, most people grow up in an environment where it's ok to live a mediocre life. You are raised in a household where you were not allowed to dream big dreams and if you did they were immediately shut down with what parents referred to as 'reality.'

Sometimes when people see you doing better than them, instead of instilling confidence in you they criticize you because they are jealous of you. The reality is, they don't have the courage and self-confidence in themselves to attempt anything extraordinary in their lives.

In return, they try to hold other people back or simply don't support their dreams. Don't allow people's opinions of you to keep you from God's best. God has amazing plans for your life.

WITH GOD ALL THINGS ARE POSSIBLE.

— MATTHEW 19:26

REFLECTION
CHECK POINT

1. What areas do you lack confidence?

_____

_____

_____

2. What ways have you displayed confidence lately?

_____

_____

_____

3. Who is someone in your life that has confidence?

_____

_____

_____

CHAPTER 2

SPEAK LIFE

A re you mindful of all the opportunities and possibilities God has for your life? The sky is the limit for you! You have the capability within you to do anything you want and God wants to fulfill the desires of your heart!

Your words have power. The power to build up or tear down. Make sure you use your words wisely.

Have you ever sat and listened to the words you use? Or even pondered on the words that others close to you share? Words are extremely powerful and can be used to speak LIFE or DEATH.

RULE OF 151

If you're the leader of an organization, make the time today to encourage and speak greatness into your employees. You could do this by complimenting their work or encouraging them when you see they may be getting frustrated.

Marcia Hoeck, author of *Step By Step Business Blueprint* shares the Rule of 151. She shares that it takes 151 times to say something for someone to believe it and before it enters the conscious minds.

- The first 50 times people don't hear you.
- The second 50 times they don't understand you.
- The third 50 times they don't believe you.
- And it isn't until they've heard it for the 151st time that they finally hear, understand, and think, *"This must be true."*

ENCOURAGE OTHERS

So, keep speaking life and encouraging those around you! The return on your investment and time will be well worth it. You will start noticing employees performing at a level never seen before. They will start going the extra mile for your organization.

You will see them doing the little things that really matter to your business' success. It's not the big things that cause an organization to fail, it is the small everyday details that seem to be overlooked at times. When your employees have the confidence and believe in themselves, they will be willing to take on the world. You will find them saying yes to everything, to every new challenge you set before them. Eventually, they will pass on what you have shared with them to create an even better culture for clients, customers and team members.

Even if you are not the leader of a company, I dare you to encourage your co-workers, family, friends, and everyone you interact with daily. I believe we were created to help others find their value and inspire them.

THE WORDS YOU SPEAK HAVE
THE POWER TO CHANGE LIVES.

Saying something as simple as, "I believe in you," can change someone's day. You will be amazed at the response you will receive. You never know what a person may be going through at that moment in life. The words you speak have the power to change lives. It can change their perspective on how they view situations they may be encountering.

STAY INSPIRED

I speak from my personal life experiences. As positive as I am, I have found myself doubting my own abilities. You see, when I was 26 years old, my father ended up passing away from cancer and it broke my heart. I was very close to my father. I had spent the last year of his life taking care of him and nurturing him.

Shortly after he passed away, I found myself in a depressed stage in life. I lacked motivation and had lost my zeal to live. During this trying season, my wife and I had our son Julian. Julian brought joy and happiness to my heart. He was one of the only things that brought a smile to my face. I was blessed with the opportunity to spend time with him as an infant.

I remember staying home with him and I cherished every moment we spent together. We watched Blue's Clues almost every day. The memories we have are priceless. I also took this time to speak life into my son even though I was mourning.

I was so grateful to God for carrying me through this time in my life. God is so amazing! He sent me an encourager, a person to speak life back into my life. God sent me a gentleman by the name of Dan Segovia. Dan has been a big blessing in my life. I was blessed to meet him during the time I worked at Clark American Checks. I looked up to Dan, I still do.

Dan entered my life at the right time, while I was still grieving the loss of my father. Dan was older than I was, but he eagerly took me under his wing and mentored me as a young man. Dan gave me a lot of Godly wisdom that opened my eyes to a new way of thinking. He shared a lot of insight on how to approach life. For instance, how to respond to situations, circumstances, and obstacles that arose in life.

The one thing that helped me the most was that Dan always spoke positivity and wisdom into my life. He would tell me, "Daniel, don't you know who you are? You are a child of the most high God. You have Christ, the hope of glory, living inside of you. You are the Temple of the Holy Spirit."

I had the pleasure of working with Dan for almost a year. During those months that we worked together, Dan always spoke confidence into my life.

Looking back now, I believe Dan had the gift of edification. He would speak words of encouragement daily into my life. God used him to help me discover my greatness and gave me a new outlook on life. I'm forever indebted to him for taking time to speak life into what appeared to be a lifeless season in my life.

THE TONGUE

HAS THE POWER OF

LIFE AND DEATH,

AND THOSE WHO LOVE IT

WILL EAT ITS FRUIT.

— PROVERBS 18:21

REFLECTION
CHECK POINT

1. What areas do you need to speak life?

_____

_____

_____

2. Do you have someone who speaks life into you?

_____

_____

_____

3. Who have you encouraged today?

_____

_____

_____

CHAPTER 3

TRIALS LEAD TO TRIUMPH

No matter what your status may be or how 'successful' you may think you are, no one is exempt from the trials of life. You have the ability to turn your trials into triumph. These events take away every ounce of happiness and joy; it seems to disappear or become buried by despair.

But if you are equipped correctly, you can use your tears to create tenacity. During these seasons of our lives, it seems like someone has stolen our right to enjoy living and to be happy; however, it doesn't have to be that way!

HEARTACHE

Some of us have gone through a terrible breakup or divorce that sucks the life out of you. Divorces and separations are never easy for the people involved, especially the children. People lose hope. They lose the desire to live.

They lose the ambition they once had to go out and conquer the world, to be somebody, to be an amazing father or mother, and to accomplish great things in their life.

LOSING A JOB

Another trial in life could be getting laid off or fired from a current position at work. After being laid off, some people think that they are never going to recover from this occurrence in their life. They lose hope, and even worse, they become discouraged with themselves. I believe, even in these current times, there are some people still saying "it isn't fair," and it's been well over a decade. They weren't able to see that they could overcome.

It's unfortunate they respond this way because the only person they are hurting is themselves, but that could be how someone reacts when they are facing difficult times. You must learn to triumph in the midst of your trials.

> DON'T
> LET LIFE
> DICTATE
> YOUR
> DECISIONS!

So perhaps, instead of focusing on being without a job, this may give you an opportunity to start your own business or go back to school to pursue a degree. If you had small children, you could use the time you are out of work to spend time with them. Don't let life dictate your decisions!

LOSING A LOVED ONE

Another trial everyone experiences is the loss of a loved one. Losing a loved one in life is never easy; I have experienced this firsthand on several occasions. It's not a feeling or life event you want anyone you care about to go through. Death is something that is guaranteed in our lives. When we do lose a loved one, many of us never get over the hurt.

Some of us continue to ask ourselves:

Why?

Why did this happen?

How can this happen to me?

They ask themselves these questions over and over, without realizing it, they develop a victim mentality. I don't mean to say it in an uncaring way, but that is how some people respond to the loss of a loved one.

I tell you from my own experiences because I have lost many loved ones in my life that were dear to me. When I was a young child I lost my mother to cancer, as an adult at the age of 26 my father passed away from it as well. The passing of my father was crushing to my soul, it broke me into pieces. I must admit, I lost my confidence and I was depressed for several weeks.

If it wasn't for God giving me the strength and courage to keep moving forward in life, I don't know where I'd be. I had the choice to continue to be sad, to feel sorry for myself, to give up on life, and to play the victim.

Now, don't get me wrong, it wasn't an easy time and there were moments when I wanted to quit. I had lost a lot of the reassurance I had as a young man. Life is never easy, but I thanked God every day for giving me the strength to press forward.

LIFE IS NEVER EASY, BUT I THANKED GOD EVERY DAY FOR GIVING ME THE STRENGTH TO PRESS FORWARD.

I remember before my dad had passed away, they informed us he only had thirty days to live. I cried out to God and I said, "If you heal my dad, I will serve you the rest of my life."

By the grace of God, my father went on to live for another year and for that I am forever grateful. It was one of the best years of my life. I could have allowed the doctor's report to have controlled of my life, but I decided I would triumph and use every moment I had left with my dad to create memories that would last a lifetime.

I have lost my mother, father, and three brothers; but I want God to get the glory in my grieving. I could easily lock myself up in a room and pout about how it's not right, or, I can do what I've been doing and thank God for the time He allowed me to have with them.

BLESSED
IS THE MAN
WHO REMAINS
STEADFAST UNDER TRIAL,
FOR WHEN HE HAS STOOD
THE TEST HE WILL RECEIVE
THE CROWN OF LIFE,
**WHICH GOD HAS
PROMISED TO THOSE
WHO LOVE HIM.**

— JAMES 1:12

REFLECTION
CHECK POINT

1. What trials are you currently facing?

_____

_____

_____

2. How can you turn your trials into triumph?

_____

_____

_____

3. How are you preparing for future trials?

_____

_____

_____

CHAPTER 4

DARE TO DREAM

The dictionary's definition of dream is imaginary events seen in the mind while sleeping. It is also a hope or wish; both can be a role in your success.

I want to encourage you today; dare to dream. If God has put a desire or idea in your mind, go after it. This goes back to living the life of mediocrity. If you won't get outside of your comfort zone, you'll never experience what life has to offer.

When kids play truth or dare with their friends, most people choose TRUTH! Why? Because they feel it is the safer option! There may be the adventurous kid that would have enough courage to take the DARE! Why stay in the safe zone? God has created you to DREAM!

When is the last time you challenged yourself to take a risk? The only way to make your dreams a reality is to transform your life! You may be required to do things you've never done! Are you willing to do what it takes?

Change the way you see yourself. Change the way you look at things. Change the way you're approaching your future, your life.

> WORK FOR WHAT YOU WANT WITH THE MINDSET OF EXPECTANCY TO CREATE WHAT YOU NEED TO FULFILL YOUR DREAMS.

Work for what you want with the mindset of expectancy to create what you need to fulfill your dreams. Just like people tell you to think outside of the box, you have to dream outside of the box too!

Be a dream chaser today. Go after your dreams with all your heart. You will amaze yourself by what you can accomplish. When you set your mind to do something and focus on it, it's as if all the powers of the universe are working for you.

POWER OF IMAGINATION

Having an imagination and dreaming go hand in hand. One of my supervisor's played an important role in helping me recreate my imagination.

It was a cold December morning and I remember all I wanted was a cup of hot chocolate. I wasn't much of a coffee drinker at the time, so, hot chocolate was my choice. As I was making my way to the hot chocolate machine, I remember our receptionist saying that Mr. Vara wanted to have a meeting with us. I was to gather all the managers together and be at his office by a certain time.

I made my way to his office, I wondered what this meeting was about. He rarely called a manager's meeting, especially one that wasn't planned. So, you could say I was excited and terrified at the same time. Everyone made their way to his office and sat down around his desk. He began by telling us about a contest Chevrolet was having for the month and how he believed we could win it.

He brought out this magazine and opened it to a page displaying a picture of a river in Colorado with an individual fly-fishing on it.

He shared that when he was younger, he always envisioned himself fly-fishing on the Colorado River. He imagined himself enjoying the beautiful outdoors and scenic views. As he continued talking to us, he said, "I believe we can do this. I believe we can win the contest. Let's make it happen!"

He asked us to use our…. imagination! I can't tell you the last time I had used my imagination. He told us to see ourselves winning just like he did when he was a child in Colorado, on the river fishing.

He said, "Imagine you've already won the contest. Envision Chevrolet presenting the award to us and the big smiles we have on our faces."

It was a powerful exercise! As the meeting continued, he told us there is power in using your imagination.

He told us another story about when he was a young man. He had just gotten into the automotive business. He said he would arrive to the dealership early in the morning and pick out two cars to go sit in. He would sit in these cars and imagine himself selling them. He would envision himself waving good bye to his customers and thanking them for their business.

Can you guess what would happen? He would sell those same cars the same day or within a week.

He explained how using your imagination in all areas of your life can be beneficial. I remember leaving the manager's meeting pumped up and ready to take on the world!

Mr. Vara also taught me a lot about integrity as well. He would always tell me, "Daniel, it's not what you do when people are watching, it's what you do when they're not." I carry those words in my heart every day. I believe this is the reason why God has blessed me and my business as much as He has.

> WHEN YOU USE YOUR IMAGINATION TO CREATE THE FUTURE YOU DESIRE, MIRACLES HAPPEN.

The following month, the results came in for the contest from Chevrolet and we were ecstatic. We won! It was an incredible feeling to share with everyone involved. Using our imagination worked. I believe it was one of the proudest moments of Mr. Vara's life.

When you use your imagination to create the future you desire, miracles happen. You can create anything you want to in life by using your imagination. All you have to do is close your eyes and envision your end goal.

* * *

The problem is, as adults we lose the creativity we had as a child. As children we would imagine ourselves playing cops and robbers. We would imagine ourselves flying and landing on the moon. We had some awesome thoughts and visions as young children. Our imagination was endless.

Activate your imagination like you did when you were a child. Don't be afraid to be a kid again. Use your imagination to help you create your future life.

Imagine you can be anything you want to be!

Imagine you are traveling all over the world!

Imagine yourself living in your dream house!

Imagine yourself helping the homeless!

There are so many ways to use your imagination; the possibilities are endless. If you have a sickness or disease, see yourself as a healthy human being.

It all starts in your mind. If you can see it in your mind, you can hold it in your hand. All products and services we use on a regular basis started as an idea. Where do you think the iPhone came from? It started as an idea in the mind of Steve Jobs. Your imagination is more powerful than you realize.

> **IF YOU CAN SEE IT IN YOUR MIND, YOU CAN HOLD IT IN YOUR HAND.**

* * *

THE WRIGHT BROTHERS

I want to remind you of the two greatest brothers in history that used their imagination and believed in the invention they wanted to create. When the Wright brothers were envisioning a machine that would fly, they did not possess the blueprint to it.

They did not have all the answers upfront, but they did have a strong imagination to create an object that would fly in the air. When the idea first came to them, they had no idea what they were going to do. All they knew was they had a desire in their heart to make such a machine. They had a determination and strong will to succeed.

They developed and engineered a plane that would fly. Which one of the brothers had his pilot's license? Neither brother possessed one. All they had was passion to build a plane and they would figure out the details later.

The fun part of the story came when it was time to land the plane. Who was going to land it? Once again, no one had ever landed a plane. None of these obstacles deterred them from succeeding! That's the power of the imagination. Their imagination gave them the intelligence they needed to land the plane safely.

*   *   *

Continue to use your imagination. Our creator created us to be creative. Don't let the gifts and talents God has given you go to waste. Use the imagination He has given you and watch everything you touch multiply!

I HAVE
A DREAM
THAT MY FOUR LITTLE CHILDREN
WILL ONE DAY LIVE IN A NATION
WHERE THEY WILL
NOT BE JUDGED BY
THE COLOR OF THEIR SKIN,
BUT BY THE CONTENT
OF THEIR CHARACTER.

— MARTIN LUTHER KING, JR.

REFLECTION
CHECK POINT

1. What were your dreams as a child compared to what they are now?

_____

_____

_____

2. What can you do today to start working toward your dreams?

_____

_____

_____

3. How have you used your imagination lately?

_____

_____

_____

CHAPTER 5

PERSISTENCE

Persistence gives you resistance against anything that is trying to interfere with your goals and makes you unstoppable. You can accomplish anything you want to in life. One of the main components to your success is going to be the amount of persistence you have. It's one of the key ingredients that is going to keep you progressing when you don't feel like it.

Persistence is going to tell you to get up the eleventh time after you have fallen ten times. Persistence is going to give you the advantage over your competitor.

You will learn to push past your pain and have strength you weren't aware you had. It's like an adrenaline rush that keeps you focused.

One of the main reasons people fail in life is because they don't develop the persistence that is required. They allow limitation, doubt, and fear to control their lives. To be successful in any endeavor you take on in life, you must have an engine named persistence. Everyone can be a dreamer and have a dream, but it takes persistence to manifest and keep that dream alive.

Imagine an airplane on the runway. As it increases in speed, persistence is the fuel that propels it into the air. A lot of people want to fly, but never take off because they don't have the persistence to keep going when a situation looks hopeless. It's the only thing you need to arise once more and face each challenge head on.

CANCER WON'T WIN

When I think of persistence, I think of my wife Mari. I think of how amazing she is. Last year, when she was diagnosed with breast cancer, it was a challenging time in her life. The average person would've given up, they would've folded. They would've quit even before the fight had started. They would have quit living life and lost all hope.

Mari persevered and fought on every day. Her faith in God gave her the inner strength she needed and carried her through this season in her life.

It showed her that she was stronger than she believed and she could accomplish whatever she set her mind on. When she was diagnosed, it was very confusing. There were many doctors giving her advice on what she should and shouldn't do. They didn't mean any harm. They were just trying to guide her down the best path they could.

Looking for another professional opinion, we went online and confused ourselves even more by reading articles. When we stopped and realized what was going on in our lives, we turned our hearts to God. He gave us the strength and determination to persevere and expect everything would turn out great.

Mari had a fighting spirit inside of her that she never knew she had. Her whole demeanor and attitude had changed; she was focused like never before. Not too long after her surgery, she was back at work. Mari was determined not to feel sorry for herself. She didn't allow herself to have a pity party and ask, "Why me?"

There were days she wasn't feeling well and I'm sure everything in her wanted to give up, but she pressed on and because of it, inspired and helped others by watching her actions.

Persistence gave her the mindset she needed to come back a lot sooner than what doctors expected. In the end, she overcame all the obstacles set before her. One of the most strenuous times on our journey was when she began receiving her radiation treatments. The treatments seemed harmless at first because you really don't feel or see any side effects they have on your body.

The treatments lasted a total of six weeks and the first three weeks went great; unfortunately, the last three weeks were a totally different story. The pain I witnessed my wife go through was devastating. It broke my heart to see my wife in such agony. Everything in me wanted to take the pain away, but Mari met the treatments head on. She WON the battle in her mind as well as in her body.

I could see the desolation in her eyes. I could see the misery she was in. She was tired from undergoing treatments every day of the week. The radiation had taken its toll on her physically and mentally. What broke my heart was that I could do nothing, but watch and pray for my wife. Without God's strength, we wouldn't have made it.

The warrior mentality Mari displayed was remarkable. She told me, "Daniel, I'm not going to allow this to beat me. I'm not going to feel sorry for myself. I know God is with me, and He is going to help me win this battle."

The moment I heard her speak those powerful words it brought tears to my eyes. It made me appreciate the person she was even more. You never want to see anyone you love experience this. There were so many miracles taking place during this time in our lives. I could see God's hand of mercy and grace guiding and protecting us.

I felt as if those last radiation treatments were ready to declare victory over my wife; however, her story doesn't end there.

The last day of radiation treatment had finally arrived. I remember it as if it was yesterday. Mari had tears in her eyes as we drove up to our driveway. As the tears made it down her cheeks she shouted, "Honey we did it, I did it! Today was my last treatment!" I will never forget the excitement, the relief, and the big smile she had on her face.

The look in her eyes as she shouted those words. At that moment in time, the burden, the weight had been lifted from her back. She had a sense of relief on her face. We said a prayer and thanked God for giving her the strength she needed to make it through those weeks. My wife was persistent and never surrendered. Mari fought the good fight of faith and won.

Her incredible story of persistence doesn't end there. You might say it was just the beginning of her heroic comeback. I recollect, about a month after Mari finished her treatments, our alarm clock went off; it was 3:30 a.m. "Did you set the alarm clock by accident?" I asked her in a puzzled manner.

In her energetic voice she replied, "Yes honey, I'm going to my body circuit workout class."

Let me explain, that class is no joke! It's an intense workout that kicks your butt. I thought she was crazy, but I could see the determination and fire in her eyes. No one was going to stop her from attending that session.

Mari is an awe-inspiring human being. The courage she displayed was remarkable. You never know how someone is going to respond to the challenges life throws at them. Seeing all the obstacles she faced and overcame was astounding. I don't know if I would have responded with the same determination and grit she had. I believe I draw a lot of my strength and motivation from her.

Every day she continues to wake up in the morning to attend her workout classes. She has a fighting spirit that pushes her to achieve more. She continues to grow and experience life in new ways. She isn't afraid to seek out new adventures or try something new. I've seen her transform into a fearless individual who embraces any challenge.

WHERE DREAMS COME TRUE

Another great example of being persistent is none other than Walt Disney himself! As the founder and creator of Disney Land and Disney World, Walt created the world's most famous cartoon character based on an animal that most people detest having in their homes, a mouse. Mickey Mouse was just a simple idea; his critics thought he was crazy.

> YOU ARE ONE NO AWAY FROM HEARING YES; REFUSE TO GIVE UP ON YOUR DREAMS!

If I was to ask you how many banks turned down Walt Disney when he was trying to acquire funding for his theme park Disney Land, what would your guess be? Walt Disney was turned down by over 300 banks on his quest to create his amazing theme park that we know today as Disney Land. You are one NO away from hearing YES; refuse to give up on your dreams!

He didn't listen to what everyone else thought. Walt was so passionate about the idea of his theme park. He didn't allow his dream to die. He had a vision of what he wanted Disney Land to be. He knew the feeling he wanted people to have when visiting it for the first time.

Because of his persistence, today we enjoy the incredible imagination of Walt Disney from the West Coast of our beautiful country all the way to the East Coast. We enjoy the creations of his imagination in the malls we go shopping at. You see a Disney Store in almost every mall in America.

Can you imagine a life without Mickey Mouse? Can you imagine a life without Disney Land? I want to challenge you today to use your imagination. If God did it for Walt Disney, he can do it for you. All you need to do is use your imagination and creativity. You have an endless supply of ideas and dreams deep inside of you.

* * *

All of us have the potential to overcome the setbacks and challenges we encounter. They make us stronger and help us develop our character. The challenges we face aren't what knock us down; it's our lack of understanding the lessons and opportunities behind them. Persistency creates consistency to fulfill a rewarding life.

YOUR TALENT IS GOD'S GIFT TO YOU. WHAT YOU DO WITH IT IS YOUR GIFT BACK TO GOD.

— LEO BUSCAGLIA

REFLECTION
CHECK POINT

1. When are you most persistent in your life?

_____

_____

_____

2. How do you keep going when life doesn't go as planned?

_____

_____

_____

3. What situation had you leaning on God's strength?

_____

_____

_____

CHAPTER 6

A CHAMPION'S ATTITUDE

I often wondered why some people would succeed in life and others wouldn't. Why do some people seem to accomplish more in life than others?

Then it hit me like a ton of bricks, your attitude determines your ALTITUDE! Did you know that there is a tool on an airplane called the ATTITUDE INDICATOR? This tool is extremely important and let's the pilot know the aircraft's orientation relative to the Earths horizon — whether it's in the air or not. I truly believe we need to have an ATTITUDE CHECK regularly. If you want to acquire a champion's attitude, you must be willing to CHECK yourself!

You must have something within yourself to make sure you are displaying a WINNING attitude, so you can soar to higher heights in your life, business, and marriage.

A positive attitude will carry you to unimaginable heights; a champion's attitude will take you even further.

FLOAT LIKE A BUTTERFLY, STING LIKE A BEE

When you hear the word champion, who or what comes to mind? My mind is automatically set on someone who has WON numerous times! Let's take Muhammad Ali for example; he's a phenomenal boxer. He has a record of 61 fights, which included 56 wins, 37 of those wins were by KO, and 5 losses. He is the only three-time lineal heavyweight champion to date. He gave more punches than he received and was the epitome of a champion in the boxing arena.

"Don't count the days; make the days count."

— Muhammad Ali

Ali also shares, "Only a man who knows what it is like to be defeated can reach down to the bottom of his soul and come up with the extra ounce of power it takes to win when the match is even." Life is going to punch you in the face. It's going to have your back against the wall, but being a champion and having a winning attitude will determine how you overcome each situation.

I truly believed it was the number of fights Muhammad Ali won that made him a champion, or was it?

AWARD WINNING SALESMAN

I began thinking of Eddie, a co-worker of mine, who had all the knowledge to be successful. I admired the way he would do a walk around on a new car and describe it like he was part of it. He had a burning passion in his heart. He would make a base model Monte Carlo look like a fully loaded one with all the bells and whistles.

I would stand at a distance, maybe fifteen to twenty feet away, just to hear him talk. He was magical. The way he moved around the car and spoke to the customers was amazing. He would have me mesmerized, with my jaw on the floor. Eddie was that good.

I would say, "Eddie, I want to sell like you when I'm done with training. You're the man!"

Looking back, I believe he thought I was just fluffing his feathers, but deep down inside I really wanted to do a new car walk around like him.

Eddie would tell me, "You're crazy Daniel! I'm not that good, there are salesman way better than me." My mind was blown away; I thought he was awesome and had the qualities of a champion!

As my first few days went by at the dealership, I soon learned that a new car walk around was only a small part of selling cars. There was so much more too it.

That following Monday we had our huge sales meeting like we did every Monday. The meeting would start, and our sales manager would ask the salesman how many units they had sold for the month.

I was in shock to find out Eddie wasn't the top salesman. "That can't be right," I said to myself. It must be wrong.

I was puzzled. One by one everyone would yell out their units sold.

David said, "Fourteen, boss."

Juan said, "Twelve, boss."

Eric said, "Eleven, boss."

Mr. Gonzales said, "Twelve sir."

As I sat back in my chair, waiting in anticipation for Eddie to yell out fifteen, it never happened.

Eddie hesitantly responded, "Three, boss."

That couldn't be right. I mean, I had spent my first few weeks admiring Eddie. I watched him perform his new car walk around with all his customers, he would kill it! He must have meant thirteen. The last salesperson yelled out his units and the meeting went on.

In the back of my mind I was still in disbelief, how could it be? I remember even asking another salesperson if the unit count for the month was correct.

"Yes, it is," he answered.

I left the sales meeting that day thinking, 'What does it take to be the best, to be the top sales person at a dealership?' I quickly learned that if I was going to succeed in the automotive industry, it all came down to my "Attitude" and not the number of sales I made.

Just because Eddie may not have had the most sales, he was still setting himself up for success because his attitude was by far one of the best I've seen in the business! Yes! Attitude is the main ingredient to a successful career in the automotive sales world.

Attitude is everything.

Without the proper attitude and mindset someone will not succeed as a salesperson in a dealership, as a matter of fact, in any sales career. That is how important having a positive state of mind is to someone's success.

POSITIVE MINDSET

To develop the characteristics of a champion, you have to have a positive mindset.

I had registered for my first sales training seminar and it was the best thing I could have done. It really changed my life, not just my work life as a sales person, but also my personal life as well. It was as if a light went off in my head and my thinking changed in a dramatic way.

It reminded me of the Bible verse Proverbs 23:7 that says, "For as he thinketh in his heart, so is he." I said to myself, "If I think positive in my heart, then my life will be positive. My sales career will be positive, everything around me will be positive."

"FOR AS HE THINKETH IN HIS HEART, SO IS HE." – PROVERBS 23:7

I was so excited about having a positive psychology I wanted to share it with everyone I knew. I wanted to inform the whole world. Some people would stare at me as if I was crazy. I was just fired up at the prospect of helping everyone discover a positive mindset.

*   *   *

> THE GREAT THING IS, IF YOU CAN CHANGE YOUR ATTITUDE, YOU CAN CHANGE YOUR LIFE.

Not everyone saw things as I did, a lot of people don't realize they possess a negative mindset. I truly believe many individuals want to change their psyche to a positive one and just don't know how. It's like they're imprisoned in a negative world.

I even had one dealership employee ask me, "Are you always this positive and happy in the morning?" Then she would say, "Sometimes you make me sick, Daniel." I just chuckled and smiled.

The great thing is, if you can change your attitude, you can change your life. I believe I've always had some positivity in my thinking, but attending the sales training seminar helped me magnify it even more. It encouraged me to focus on being positive every second of every day; it's a choice.

Some people focus on the glass being half empty, while others concentrate on the glass being half full. I focus on the glass having something in it and if someone is thirsty enough, they'll drink what is available.

SMILE

As you start developing a "Champion's Attitude" you will start seeing life from a new perspective. You will feel better about yourself. You will feel better about your career. Having the right attitude elevates your life to a higher level. The bottom line is your life will dramatically improve in all facets.

You are probably thinking right now, how do I create a champion's attitude? The one most important thing to start off with is, you need to know that your attitude determines how you live your life. It determines the quality of your life as well; if you are not happy with your life you need to change your attitude.

It's simple to get started. How? Start smiling! Yes, start smiling more and more. The more you smile, the better you will feel. Smiling will give you an instantaneous attitude boost. Try smiling for a minute while you think of a happy memory or the very last thing which made you smile. It will make you feel positive. It takes less muscle to smile than it does to frown, so turn your frown upside down and smile.

Smiling releases endorphins and serotonin in your body. They are known as the 'make you feel good' hormones. There is so much power in a smile, it can make or break a company. You don't believe me? Think about this for a moment. What if you had a manager or boss that came into work every day grumpy and not smiling.

Would you want to work for him? My guess would be you wouldn't and after a couple of months you would probably start looking for another job or ask for a transfer to another department. That is how powerful a smile can be.

Smiles are contagious! When you smile at someone most of the time they will smile back. I challenge you tomorrow to walk into your school or job and smile.

Observe the chain reaction it will create. When people start smiling it makes the next person, then the next person smile. A smile has the capability to change your life and create a champion's attitude.

LAUGH

Once you have mastered the power of the smile, laugh more. Laugh in the morning. Laugh during the day. You need to find a way to create more laughter in your life. Laughter is good medicine for the soul. It helps you smile more and creates a positive attitude.

A positive attitude makes you a happier person, it helps make you stronger. Developing a champion's attitude increases your chances of success in any endeavor.

> YOU WERE NOT CREATED TO BE MEDIOCRE, YOU WERE CREATED TO EXCEL.

A positive attitude makes you more creative; it gives you the ability to think of awesome ideas. It can help you make wiser decisions in every area of your life. Nothing is carved in stone, change your attitude today. Be more positive. You were not created to be mediocre, you were created to excel. It is a proven fact, the happier a person is, the longer and healthier they will live.

A positive mindset pays great dividends. You start attracting positive situations into your life. Suddenly, you get promoted. Suddenly, someone blesses you unexpectedly. Suddenly, the problem that was lingering overhead is resolved. That is the power of having positivity in your life, you become a magnet for everything beneficial.

ATTITUDE OF GRATITUDE

Live a life of gratitude. Be grateful for everything you have and all that God has given you from the time He gives you, down to the last dime you have. We are all on borrowed time, so be grateful for the job you have, your family, and just being able to experience life.

I had a friend that was never happy. He always focused on the negative in his life. The same way you attract more positive opportunities in your life with a positive attitude, is the same way you attract more negative ones into your life with a negative attitude. He would always say things such as, "When I get a better job I will be happy," or "When I save more money I will be happy." People need to realize that materialistic items and money do not buy happiness. You must make your decision daily and choose to be grateful for what you do have and work toward the things you desire.

I remember on one occasion, when we were enjoying a bright sunny day swimming, I asked how everything was going? I should have never asked; a negative attitude always focuses on the negative. He literally went off on a fifteen-minute rant on how bad his job was, and how hard life has been. He continued by explaining to me that nothing ever works out for him and his vehicle had just broken down. The more negativity you focus your energy on, the more you are going to attract to yourself.

My point is this, we as people can use our faith in a negative way. Instead of using our faith to improve our lives and believe in God's best, we use it in fear. Don't use your energy and faith to attract the negative circumstances that you don't want to encounter.

It saddens me to see people being ungrateful. I learned long ago that a person must want to change their life. They must want it for themselves. The question is, are they going to truly commit to improving their life and stop going around the same mountain over and over?

LIVE A POSITIVE LIFE

We carry so many emotions. Many of them are buried deep down in our souls. Let your soul be healed today. Allow God's light to shine through your heart and give you the joy you want in your life. It's never easy, but you can do it. Don't listen to that little voice in the back of your mind. Your champion's attitude is counting on you.

Life is so much better when you have a positive attitude. You feel better about yourself and you start loving yourself more. There are always going to be challenges in your life. Every morning the little voice in your head is going to try to lure you down the wrong path. It is going to tell you not to get out of bed to workout. It will try and convince you not to exercise today.

I recommend that every time the negative voice starts to speak to you, you find a Scripture that will remind you who you are, a Scripture that will remind you what you are capable of accomplishing.

VIRTUALLY NOTHING
IS IMPOSSIBLE
IN THIS WORLD IF
YOU JUST PUT
YOUR MIND TO IT
AND MAINTAIN A
POSITIVE
ATTITUDE.

— LOU HOLTZ

REFLECTION
CHECK POINT

1. What are you most grateful for today?

_____

_____

_____

2. Do you practice gratitude daily?

_____

_____

_____

3. What ways can you work toward thinking more positively?

_____

_____

_____

CHAPTER 7

HELP MY UNBELIEF

Some of us believe in big dreams for our friends. It is great to support other people's dreams and goals, but I want you to believe it for yourself. Start believing you can achieve the dreams you have for your life. You deserve the best in life. Do not be intimidated! Do not be scared! Go after the dreams you have in your heart.

> GO AFTER THE DREAMS YOU HAVE IN YOUR HEART.

You are meant to live a blessed life so that you may be a blessing to the people around you. God wants to bless you. God wants you to prosper. God wants your cup to overflow. Expect God's best for your life; receive His favor!

FEAR OF FAILURE

God has so much in store for you. You can't even begin to imagine what he wants to do for your life. The problem is, we allow the opinion of other people to set limitations on our lives. It's like they preset the thermostat on what level of success we will obtain. Make up your mind right now to raise your thermostat to a higher level. You may need to associate with people living life at a higher frequency than you.

I am here to inform you that you are equipped and talented enough to live a spectacular life. You have all the resources you need to succeed. I want you to forget about all the failures from your past. Erase them from your mind and start imagining the amazing life God has waiting for you. It is overflowing with blessings.

You need to do yourself a favor when you start envisioning the life you want to live in five years. Do not base it on your current circumstances. The truth is, you can create any future life you want. You don't need to have all the answers within you. Don't allow fear to keep you from getting started. Fear prevents people from taking action and pursuing their passion. You can not fail if you never try and you can never succeed if you never fail.

YOUSIF'S STORY

Imagine being told you can't run, play outside with the other children, live an ordinary childhood or that you can't go to school because you might die. Imagine being told everyday of your life you were not normal.

I had the pleasure of meeting Yousif this year at McCombs Ford West while conducting a sales training workshop. Those words are exactly what he was told for more than half of his life. The more I conversed with him and heard his story, the more amazed I was at all the things he had overcome. Yousif was diagnosed with a rare heart condition, which kept him from doing all the normal activities that normal children do.

Every day, Yousif was reminded of the daily pastimes he could not participate in by his mother. Every day, he was reminded of his physical limitations set by his heart condition. Every day, he was reminded that he had an illness. Every day, he was being programed with the mindset that he would never live a healthy and prosperous life.

As the days passed by, Yousif found himself living a life filled with frustrations and restrictions. He found himself at the hospital almost every month because he started believing what he was being told by his mother and the physicians. He started believing in his mind that his medical conditions were worse than they were.

At the age of around nine years old, his health condition worsened and Yousif soon found himself at home and no longer attending school. His health had deteriorated so much that his heart valve was closing and shrinking at a faster pace than originally anticipated by his doctors. They soon found that his heart enlarged from the lack of blood and oxygen needed to perform daily activities.

Once again, Yousif was reminded of his illnesses and being advised of his physical limitations by his doctors and mother. He soon underwent surgery to repair his heart valve to give him some sort of normal life. Yousif lived his childhood with the mindset that he would never be able to perform and do the everyday activities normal people do.

Then at the age of sixteen everything changed for Yousif, he started reading and retraining his mind. He started believing he could be anything he wanted to be. He transformed and renewed his thinking. Everything the doctor and his mother had told him his entire life was being challenged by the books he was reading. Yousif had a new belief. Yousif was a new creation.

It is amazing what the mind can do when it is reprogrammed to accomplish activities it has never accomplished before. Yousif started participating in all the pastimes he had always wanted to do as a child. He found himself walking without worrying about getting tired and fatigued.

After a couple of months, Yousif challenged himself to start running and exercising. He never imaged or dreamt he would be as active as he was. He cried tears of joy. Yousif's life story was being rewritten with every successful day he had. He was experiencing a life of freedom and happiness. His life reminds me of Napoleon Hill's famous quote, "Whatever the mind can believe it can achieve."

At the age of eighteen, the real miracle started taking place in Yousif's life. Yousif was scheduled to go visit his doctor as normal, but to his doctor's surprise Yousif's heart was operating like a normal heart. He couldn't believe the arteries were not shrinking any longer and getting smaller. They were the same size as Yousif's prior visit.

He thought to himself, there is no way this could have happened. "What have you been doing Yousif?", asked the doctor. Yousif replied, "I have been reading a lot of books, and I believe I can be normal like any other human being. I believe I can live a normal life."

From that moment on, Yousif lived a normal and healthy life. It just goes to show us when you believe something with all your heart and with all your soul, it will come to pass. Your mind is so powerful it can create the life you desire. Change your beliefs and your life follows.

I was so fascinated by Yousif's story, every time I went to McCombs Ford West I would speak to him about his life. His story really inspired me and showed me that we can create the life of our dreams. You can think it into existence. The problem is, most people focus on the problem and what they don't have instead of focusing on the good and what they do have.

LIMITING BELIEFS

If there is one lesson I have learned from Yousif's story, it is that our thoughts become things. Our thoughts become the reality we live in. Our thoughts become our future life. If you want to change your future, you need to change your thoughts. You need to change what you focus on. Changing your limiting beliefs is not an easy task to accomplish, but it can be done. You can reprogram your mind to obtain the life you want.

The Bible tells us there is power in the words that we speak. It teaches us that our tongue is powerful. This is very true. The words we speak daily create the future and beliefs we have for ourselves and for our lives.

If you want to change your life, if you want to change your future, pay attention to the words you are saying every day. The words you are saying are creating the life you live. Don't go around talking about your problems. Don't go around talking about what you don't have. Don't go around focusing on the negative situations in your life.

I challenge you to shift your thinking. I encourage you to change your beliefs. I want you to focus on the future you want for yourself. I want you to envision the future you want for your family. I want you to see yourself working in the career you desire. Envision the life you want to have in five years. What does your future look like?

If your current beliefs are telling you, "That would never happen." Tell yourself, "It can happen for me. I deserve God's best. God's favor is with me." Tell yourself that every day. Don't allow your old beliefs to keep you from the future God has planned for you.

Tell yourself, "I will have the career I desire. I will have the future life I want. I am buying my dream car. I am buying my dream house." There is power in the words you speak every day. Create the future you want by speaking it into existence.

Alter your limiting beliefs and start telling yourself you can accomplish anything you put your mind to.

With the correct mindset and beliefs, you can succeed in life. You can conquer the world. I am here to let you know you were not created to be average. You were not created to be mediocre. You were created for greatness! Do not settle for average. No one said it was going to be easy, but it will be worth it in the long run. You have an amazing future waiting for you.

THE POWER OF I AM

"I AM" are two of the most powerful words in the universe. The words that follow them become your reality. I can't tell you how many people I hear speaking negatively over their lives. There is power in your words, so watch what you say carefully. I want you to start declaring these words over your life daily:

I am accomplishing everything I desire.

I am creating a life of abundance.

I am living in my dream home.

I am buying my wife her dream car.

I am blessing the homeless and the needy.

I am wealthy. I am a cheerful giver.

Once you start focusing on the goals you have, you are going to be amazed at the progress you are going to make. All of your energy, all of your strength, and all of your power is going to go where your focus is. It is going to allow you to achieve your

NEVER
SETTLE FOR
WHAT YOU
DON'T
WANT IN
YOUR LIFE.

dreams faster. It's like taking a magnifying glass and multiplying the power that is behind you.

It is going to accelerate your future. What should have taken you fifteen to twenty years to accomplish, because of your focus and beliefs you have in place now, you will accomplish in seven to ten years. Always remember you have the power in your mind to create the future you desire.

Never settle for what you don't want in your life. There is so much more to life than you can imagine. By changing your beliefs and removing the limitations you had on yourself, you are going to create a life full of joy and happiness. You will start living a life of purpose, one full of blessings.

DEFEATED ELEPHANT

An elephant is one of the largest animals, but can be bound by a rope and stake tied to its foot. At a very young age, captive elephants are trained to believe they cannot break away from the rope. They are conditioned to believe the rope is stronger than them.

These massive land animals, at any time, could break away from their restraints, but they have been trained to believe that they can't. They remain limited in their abilities.

How many of us, like captive elephants, go through life confined to a belief system which restrains us from attempting a new endeavor? We stay confined to our comfort zones, never stepping into the realm of the unknown. How many of us are being held back by old beliefs which no longer serve us? How many of us have avoided trying something new because of a limited belief?

When you were younger, something could have prevented you from believing you could do something. But when you learn more, you can do more. There is NOTHING you can't do!

YOU AREN'T YOUR PARENTS

Are someone else's limiting beliefs of you keeping you constrained? Do not allow their view of you to keep you from being your best. It may even be your own parents trying to keep you from achieving your heart's desire. Your parents' beliefs were to live simple lives and to never take risks. They were programmed since they were kids to believe they had limitations. "Things aren't so bad. Why do you want to attempt something crazy like that?" They tell you, "You are doing good where you are." These are just a few examples of the limiting beliefs they may possess.

Parents can keep us from being the best version of ourselves. They can keep us from expanding our wings and venturing out. They can teach us to be afraid, to live in a box of restrictions. Do not allow the limiting beliefs of your parents or of anyone else to keep you from being all that God created you to be. Remember, your life has a purpose and destiny. You will never fulfill your destiny doing work you despise.

Don't allow the limiting beliefs in your mind to keep you chained up. If you're currently unhappy at your job, it might be your heart speaking to you, your inner passion dying to come out. Find a career where you love what you do. Don't allow these thoughts to keep you in a cage your entire life. You weren't born to be in a cage. You were born to make a difference in people's lives.

PURSUE YOUR PASSION

I challenge you today to step outside the comfort zone in your mind and start creating your new life. Find your passion in life. Passion gives you an advantage over others. Passion gives you energy! When you find your passion, you will realize it isn't work.

When God puts a dream in your heart, you don't have to have all the answers as to how you're going to accomplish it. All you have to do is believe it can and will happen. You must believe that it will come to pass. Don't focus on the resources you don't have. Don't allow your current circumstances to dictate your life.

Limited beliefs about ourselves and negative views of ourselves often keep us from following the dreams we have in our heart.

I often think of my friend Joseph. Since we were young, Joseph would always say he was going to be successful in life, that he was going to make something of himself. He always pushed himself to a higher standard. The great thing about that is Joseph always challenged me to have bigger aspirations also. To have dreams of my own.

He always believed we were the best, that we could accomplish anything in life. As a young manager at a food chain he always tried to exceed the goals that were set before him, not just achieve them. He would always tell me, "You need to strive to be better Danny." He motivated me to go above and beyond in everything I did. Joseph joined the Army and went on to have a great military career. He had a chance to travel the world and eventually he met his beautiful wife and started his family.

Now looking back, I believe he was successful because of his beliefs. Joseph believed he could accomplish anything he set his mind to. I am so proud of him. He now resides in El Paso, Texas and has a very successful career as a firefighter. He believed in his heart that he could be one of the best firefighters in El Paso. The great thing is, he has done an amazing job for his community as a firefighter. As I was reflecting on our lives, I realized that the years go by so fast. His retirement is right around the corner.

I could not believe it, when we talked on the phone a couple of months back, we were discussing him possibly moving to San Antonio. One thing I always remember about Joseph is he always pushed us to be better. He challenged the status quo. Joseph is an amazing individual, a friend you always want to have in your life. He always encourages you and reminds you to reach for the stars, that you can achieve anything you put your mind to. He would say, "Danny you can do it!"

Even though I do not see him all the time, I think of him often. I think of the great memories we had growing up in San Marcos and being dreamers.

If you need a word of encouragement today, I am here to let you know it is never too late to begin living out your dreams. All you need to do is take some form of action and get started. Surround yourself with people that are going to support the vision you have for your future. There is a definite advantage when you surround yourself with people which have the same drive and desire as you do. What are you waiting for? Replace those limiting beliefs in your mind with ones that will serve you.

WE LEARN
OUR BELIEF SYSTEMS
AS VERY LITTLE CHILDREN,
AND THEN WE MOVE
THROUGH LIFE
CREATING EXPERIENCES
TO MATCH OUR BELIEFS.
LOOK BACK IN YOUR
OWN LIFE AND
NOTICE HOW OFTEN
YOU HAVE GONE THROUGH
THE SAME EXPERIENCE.

— LOUISE L. HAY

REFLECTION
CHECK POINT

1. What are you passionate about that brings you the most joy?

_____

_____

_____

2. What is keeping you from doing what you love?

_____

_____

_____

3. What beliefs do you struggle with?

_____

_____

_____

CHAPTER 8

LIVE TO FORGIVE

I want to take you back to the analogy of skydiving. Once someone leaps off of the plane and into the air, they experience a weightlessness. Now just imagine if you added so much weight that it took away from the experience or caused serious issues? The same thing applies with forgiveness.

People go around carrying so much additional weight that they don't have to! Let's keep the analogy of flying — this time, with a carry on and additional luggage. An aircraft has to have the weight proportioned correctly to have a successful flight. If weight was not distributed the correct way, it could cause issues. Not forgiving someone is additional baggage you weren't meant to carry. It keeps you from performing at your peak; it slows you down.

Take a moment to think about it. If you carried extra weight around with you, would you be able to live life to the fullest? No, because it would limit you from doing certain activities in your personal and professional life. You wouldn't be able to walk as fast as you would like. You wouldn't be able to take a bicycle ride in the park. You wouldn't be able to do certain things because you're literally carrying this weight on your shoulders and trying to balance it.

You might be saying, "That's ridiculous, that's not true," but many people you are close to live this way every day. They had a situation in their life that hurt them and without realizing it they have allowed unforgiveness to settle in their heart. It's a powerful force in our world. I've witnessed it destroy families, lifelong friendships, and professional careers. I have seen it consume and eat away at a person's life from the inside.

* * *

One day, I walked into our mechanic shop at one of the dealerships I worked at and people were yelling from every direction. Two of our employees were having a heated conversation, yelling from one side of the shop to the other. They were two brothers working together that despised each other.

You could still see the frustration and anger in their countenance, even after we calmed them down. You could see all of their emotions through the gestures they made. It was an intense moment.

After we separated them, they made their way back to their work areas in the mechanic shop, but you could still feel the tension in the air.

I made my way to one of the brothers and asked him, "What's going on? What's happening here?"

He told me things from their personal life, issues that they had in the past. He continued to explain situations that had happened five to six years ago.

I thought to myself, "Wow! Some people carry these feelings and emotions around for years, they don't let them go." I continued to listen. They were harboring so many unhealthy emotions that had built up over the years. You could feel the anger, resentment, and bitterness as he told me his side of the story.

I said, "I understand. Take a couple of minutes to relax and breathe. Better yet, why don't you take an early lunch to calm down and get away from this place for an hour or so?"

It was a crazy morning and I still had to discuss what had happened with the other brother. I could feel the negative vibes as I walked up to his stall. I gathered his side of the story. I came to find that he'd been carrying these emotions of anger and bitterness for some time now.

"But it's not fair," he complained. He brought up issues from five, even ten years ago. As I stood there listening to him, I was in awe of how much hatred he had in his heart.

When you don't forgive someone, that seed of unforgiveness is planted in your heart. It takes up residence without you realizing it, and as time goes on that seed continuously grows. It breeds unhealthy emotions, which doesn't add value to your life. These negative emotions transform your heart.

In this case, that small seed that started as unforgiveness between the brothers grew into resentment. They began resenting one another and as that seed continued to grow, they became bitter.

Once these gentleman were able to see things differently, they were able to put their pride to the side and work toward rebuilding their relationship which would benefit their family in ways they would never even know.

SEEDS OF HATRED

Once that happens, that tiny seed turns into hatred and you go through life with hatred in your heart. The last thing you want in your life is to carry hatred with you every day. When those negative feelings and emotions invade your soul, it leaks from one relationship to another.

Have you ever met a person that was just angry at the world? They always seemed mad or unhappy about everything in their life? You could see it in them.

You really don't know what's wrong, but you can sense that there's something bothering them. Well, that's what happened. They allowed a minuscule seed of unforgiveness to grow, blossom, and harden their heart.

Before you know it, just like when someone gains weight, it's there. The seed of unforgiveness becomes a plant, rooted deep into your soul. Having contempt in your heart makes you an angry person. No matter what the circumstances are, you find yourself getting angry.

Then you become short tempered, which seeps into your relationships with your wife/husband, friends, co-workers and your children. You'll find yourself alone because nobody really wants to be associated with your negativity.

BITTER TO BETTER

Take a moment to reflect on your life, we've all had that one coworker that nobody wanted to be around because everything they said was negative. Everything they comment on brings people down, everything they say is not edifying nor encouraging. It doesn't make work better, much less any other situation.

I encourage you to spend some time alone in a quiet room to meditate and ask yourself, ask God, "Are there areas in my heart where I have unforgiveness?"

The last thing you want to be is that bitter, impassioned person that no one wants to be around. You were created to bring joy, happiness, and excitement into people's lives. Sometimes a person is blinded by their pain and they don't even realize this is going on in their life.

ANGRY AND HURT

A few years ago, I was short tempered and I couldn't understand what the cause of it was. One day, I got so upset that my eyes watered from all the animosity from deep down inside of me. I got in my car and drove off to cool down. I cried out to God to help me, to take the anger inside me and I ended up at a store.

I found myself at a bookstore called the Scripture Stall. I entered, not fully understanding why I was there. As I made my way towards the back of the bookstore, I came across a book that was about anger and the causes of it. It immediately caught my attention so I grabbed the book and began to read. Then, I cried.

One of the pages of the book asked, "Who are you angry at? Who have you not forgiven?" After reading these questions repeatedly, I sat down and prayed. I asked God, "Who have I not forgiven?" I cried out to him to reveal them to me. "Who?"

That day, God revealed to me that I was angry with my father. I'd been carrying it with me for many years without knowing! I was shocked. I wanted to know the cause.

The Lord enlightened me. My dad had gone home to be with Him five years prior. I knew I had to forgive him, but how?

EPHESIANS 4:32, "BE KIND TO ONE ANOTHER, TENDER HEARTED, FORGIVING EACH OTHER JUST AS GOD IN CHRIST ALSO HAS FORGIVEN YOU."

As I sat there crying, I asked God to release the unforgiveness in my heart, to help me forgive him for the memories I had as a child. I wept and wept. I released the emotions of unforgiveness in my heart, and I forgave him. Instantaneously, I felt the burden being lifted from my shoulders.

It was like a weight was released and this sense of suppressed pain was removed. At that moment, I remembered a Scripture I read, Ephesians 4:32, "Be kind to one another, tender hearted, forgiving each other just as God in Christ also has forgiven you." We must forgive to be forgiven.

I had already been a Christian for a couple of years and as I thought of that Scripture I said, "Who am I not to forgive my father after everything I've done?" God forgave me; I put my head down and cried.

After I left the Scripture Stall, I wasn't sure how I felt. I knew I felt different, even relieved, but I didn't understand what happened. The following weeks were incredible! My wife could see the difference in who I was and who I was becoming. She commented, "Honey, you just look happier."

FORGIVE FOR YOURSELF

That's what happens when you choose to forgive; it brings life into your soul. And remember this, when you forgive someone, you're not doing it for their benefit. You're doing it for yourself. Forgiveness frees your mind, body and soul. Forgiveness removes the shackles that were holding you back.

The Bible makes it clear that if we don't forgive, how can we expect God to forgive us? Many of us go through life without experiencing true joy. I'm not talking about living the extravagant life of the rich and famous, but the little things.

No matter if you drive a $5,000, a $20,000 or a $60,000 Corvette, that's not going to bring you true fulfillment in life. True happiness comes from being able to forgive others and enjoy the little things with those you love.

DIVORCE CAUSES PAIN

Experiencing life with a heart freed of unforgiveness is a blessing. What comes to mind is divorce. Divorce is a hard situation to encounter in life. It can be devastating to everyone involved. It doesn't only affect the spouses.

It also shatters the hearts of the children. People don't realize how much pain and suffering a child goes through. It has a huge psychological effect because it interrupts their lives.

I encourage you to release the unforgiveness you have towards your spouse, ex-husband, or ex-wife. In some cases, people carry a lot of baggage from previous relationships into their new one. That's why several second marriages struggle or don't make it. The emotions a person carries can keep them from loving a person the way they should.

Many people carry similar feelings and emotions in their life that I held against my father. The irony is, people don't even realize it. I'll tell you, if you carry those emotions from one relationship to another, eventually they will disclose themselves. At first, you don't see them because in a new relationship you're on cloud nine.

You're thankful because you have a new partner and friend. When the first sign of adversity comes, those emotions and feelings reveal themselves. You start putting up walls and become defensive. Then, from one moment to the next, you may begin disengaging yourself from the relationship.

We commence building these mental barriers because we remember the pain from past relationships. These emotions keep us from living the best lives that we possibly can. They keep us from experiencing the excitement of growing together as a couple and living a life of contentment and satisfaction.

Today, take a moment for yourself. Sit on the side of your bed and release the unforgiveness you have towards your ex-husband or ex-wife. You'll thank yourself for it. It will free you to live an exuberant life filled with blessings. Like I mentioned before, you're not doing it for your ex-spouse, you're doing it for you.

You might be saying, "Daniel, you don't know what they did to me. You don't understand what they put me through. You don't know how many times they cheated on me. You don't know how many times they lied to me." Forgiving someone may not be easy, but it's worth it!

You might've been verbally abused for years and it took a toll on you. It took a toll on your mind, soul, your very being. One thing I will tell you, there is power in forgiveness. Open your heart. Open your mind. Open your soul. Ask God to give you the strength and courage to forgive.

> FORGIVING SOMEONE MAY NOT BE EASY, BUT IT'S WORTH IT!

Your miracle is waiting for you. Your new heart is waiting for you. For God himself has given me a new heart and for that, I am forever grateful. Forgiveness is a process; I challenge you today to let go and let God.

FORGIVE,
AND YOU WILL BE
FORGIVEN.

— LUKE 6:37

REFLECTION
CHECK POINT

1. Who do you need to forgive?

_____

_____

_____

2. Is there anything you've done that you haven't forgiven yourself?

_____

_____

_____

3. When is the last time you forgave someone that hurt you?

_____

_____

_____

CHAPTER 9

INSPIRE

Inspiration comes in many forms. I have been blessed to be inspired everyday by someone I hold dear to my heart. One never knows where their daily inspiration will be coming from or what exactly that source may look like.

If you were to tell me when my son was born, that he would be the one inspiring me in life, I would have disagreed. The chances of that happening are slim to none, considering I was the father and he was the son. After all, it's the responsibility of the parent to be the one motivating and inspiring his son.

My son Julian has grown into a person that I am very proud of and that I deeply admire. They say the apple doesn't fall far from the tree, but in this case, I must give all the glory to God for making him the person he is today.

It was around two years ago today, on a beautiful summer day, that Julian challenged me in the weight room. He implied that he would be bench pressing more weight than I was.

He said, "Dad, by the end of the summer, I will be bench pressing a lot more weight than you. Watch and see!"

My reply to him was, "Son you must be crazy. Let's put a friendly wager on it and you will see it's not going to happen."

So that summer day, the details of the wager were set and there was no turning back. Julian had until the end of October to bench press more weight than me.

I took this very personal, because bench pressing is my favorite workout routine when it comes to free weights. Without even realizing it at the time, he awakened a side of me that had been dormant for quite some time. Julian inspired me! By challenging me, he ignited a fire that's still burning today.

To my surprise, Julian was challenging himself and working out like never before. Since it was summer, he didn't have to attend school and had hours of free time for himself. I told him, "Son, anyone can work out when they have all summer off, the real challenge will come when school starts, and you have to make time to go the gym. Will you be able to do it when you will need to balance out life, school, and work? No pressure."

BY CHALLENGING ME, HE IGNITED A FIRE THAT'S STILL BURNING TODAY.

Then one September morning while I was warming up at the gym, guess who comes walking in at 5:00 a.m.? You guessed it, Julian did! For the first time in my life I saw him developing into a young man, the young man God created him to be. He was coming of age and was determined to bench press more than me. It opened my eyes to the fact that he was not a little boy any more.

It was like God used him to wake up another side of myself that I never knew I had. My son, my little king, as I call him, inspired me to be better. I took Julian seriously. I soon found myself working out harder, doing an extra rep here and there.

I found myself doing an extra five to eight minutes of cardio per workout to stay ahead of him. It was truly inspiring to see him push and apply himself daily, to achieve his goal of bench pressing more than me. Julian inspired me to work out and apply myself like never before.

You might be wondering, who won the bet? It was closer than I imagined it would be. I ended up winning the wager. But in all reality, I won a whole lot more than anticipated. I won the fact that my inspiration to improve my life came from my son. Julian inspired and continues to inspire me each day.

He always reminds me of a quote I told him as a boy, "Winners never quit and quitters never win." What more could a father ask for from his son?

ENCOURAGE A STRANGER

In this life, you will have many choices to make as a person. You will have the choice to inspire and uplift someone daily. I believe that God will put people in front of you intentionally every day of your life to encourage them.

Many of those people that are going to cross your path are meant for you to inspire. They are there for you to help improve their life in some shape or form. You might not understand everything, but that's okay. Just know, when some stranger walks up to you out of nowhere, it might just be a divine appointment God has sent to you.

They may need a word of inspiration at that exact moment in their life. You see, everybody needs to be inspired. Everyone needs to be reassured that things are going to be ok. You never know what a person might be going through.

They may have a loved one that received some bad news about having a sickness or disease. They may have lost their job and have no idea how they're going to pay their bills or make it through life. They may have just received some form of bad news that sucked the life out of them.

> YOU NEVER KNOW WHAT A PERSON MIGHT BE GOING THROUGH.

So, before you shrug somebody off that crosses your path today, take time to ask yourself if there is anything you can do for this person. You'll be surprised at what you're capable of doing. You may be asking what you could possibly give to anyone and thinking that you don't know what to do. You may think you don't have anything to give. The reality of it is that you can do more than you know. We as human beings have something to give that's deep inside of us.

When God created us in His image and likeness He deposited a huge dose of love inside of us. That love is meant to be given and shared with the people around us. The beautiful thing about life is that the more love and inspiration you give, the more you receive.

I've learned that when I'm feeling down and out and I need a word of encouragement, I love to go out there and make something happen for someone else. Even if it's something as simple as buying them a cup of coffee or buying someone lunch.

Take some form of action and let a friend or family member know you care. It can even be a total stranger that God placed in front of you. Act and you will be amazed at the dividends it will bring into your life.

BE AN INSPIRATION OF LOVE

Love is one of the greatest gifts in the world. I guarantee you, when you demonstrate the love of Christ to someone, it will transform their life and a transformation will take place. That is the power of inspiration, it changes the direction of a person's life for the better. Step out of your comfort zone and show someone you care today.

> LOVE IS THE GREATEST GIFT IN THE WORLD.

When you do something meaningful for another person, it makes you feel better as a human being. What you make happen for others, God will make happen for you. The more seeds you sow in life that are good, inspiring, and edifying, the more good you will receive. It's the law of sowing and reaping. Be like a farmer and sow tons of seeds of inspiration and watch something magical happen.

SHAKE IT OFF

One of the most inspiring individuals I've ever met is William Johnson II. I had the pleasure of meeting Mr. Johnson at the very first dealership where I worked. Mr. Johnson was a marvelous individual and sales manager. He always inspired me to be the best in every aspect of life. I admired how he always smiled throughout the day and didn't allow circumstances to alter his mood. Mr. Johnson, also known as 'G' never allowed the little things to ruin his groove.

I remember asking him, "How do you not let anything affect you 'G'?"

His response was, "You have to be like a duck and let the water roll off of your back."

The first time I heard that saying I thought he was crazy. Like a duck? But the more I thought about it, I recall seeing a duck put it's head in the water and when it came back up, it shook its body and titled his head upward. It didn't let the environment affect him. So, I had to learn to SHAKE IT OFF!

The more we worked together, the more I realized that Mr. Johnson was right. When something challenging comes along in life we have a choice to allow it to alter our state of mind for the negative or the positive. He would always keep his composure and choose a positive state of mind. He would be just like a duck and allow the water to flow down his back. It seemed like nothing would get under his skin. I had the pleasure of working with him for six years and I enjoyed our time together.

I remember one morning I arrived at the dealership and I just wasn't feeling it. It was one of those rare funky mornings when you don't want to get out of bed. I walked in with a discouraged look. You could say I was feeling sorry for myself and I wasn't motivated at all. However, as soon as I saw Mr. Johnson, I knew everything was going to be ok. He always seemed to draw the best out of people.

He would tell me, "God has already taken care of all your needs my brother. Everything is going to be alright."

Mr. Johnson always said the right words at the right time. He would alter the course of my day for the better. Looking back at it, he actually helped guide me to where I am today. There's a lot of him in me. Many of the qualities I have as a manager and leader, I learned from him. True inspiration lasts for a lifetime. He was a man of inspiration.

I believe true inspiration comes from the heart, from within a person's soul. It comes from their most inward being. Inspiration has the power to change a person's life. It has the power to alter any situation that you may encounter. You may be feeling defeated at the present moment, with no hope in sight. It looks like there's no light at the end of the tunnel. That's when inspiration comes along and lifts you up. It carries you on its shoulders and whispers into your ear to arise and conquer the day, conquer your circumstances.

You see yourself getting stronger and stronger. Inspiration strengthens your feelings, your emotions and how you view your circumstances. It can take you from the lowest valley to the highest mountain top. Confidence takes you from losing all hope to having the kind of faith that can move mountains! Never stop believing; never stop hoping.

Wake up every day with inspiration in your heart. Wake up and choose to inspire the people you communicate with daily. Inspire their heart. Inspire their soul. Inspire their mind. Your words will breathe new life into them. You have the power to inspire!

CREATIVE THINKING
INSPIRES IDEAS.
IDEAS
INSPIRE CHANGE.

— BARBARA JANUSZKIEWICZ

REFLECTION
CHECK POINT

1. Who inspires you?

_____

_____

_____

2. Who have you inspired?

_____

_____

_____

3. How has inspiration been beneficial in your life?

_____

_____

_____

CHAPTER 10

WIN THE MORNING

I t's a beautiful crisp morning. There's dew on the grass, the air is brisk, God's painting is displayed in the sky as the sun rises. I have one simple question, is your day planned for success? Most of us wake up every morning and we press the snooze button, not once, not twice, but three times! Some people even set a reminder for the alarm clock to remind them to get up.

Then we find ourselves running behind, rushing to get dressed, rushing to get the kids to school, and rushing to get ourselves to work on time. In this chaotic environment, you set yourself up for failure and the next thing you know, you find yourself stressed out and overwhelmed.

You pull up to a red traffic light. You notice the light is taking forever and you become frustrated. The longer the light takes to turn green, the more irritated you become. Then, you get another red traffic light and now you're getting angry, maybe even furious.

You begin tapping your fingers on the steering wheel impatiently. You look at your watch and tap your fingers faster.

You look at your watch again and finally the light turns green. As you're making your way down the boulevard, guess what, you catch another red light. Now you're irate! To think, all of this could have been avoided if you would've planned your morning for success.

You finally make it to work, not in the best of moods. You walk into the office and your co-worker smiles and says, "Good morning, how are you doing this morning?"

And you're like, "Terrible. I caught every red light, nothing seems to be going right this morning."

Pause for a moment and think about everything you just read. Whose fault was it? Who is the person responsible for the way your morning went? The answer to these questions is, you. You are responsible for you. I just described to you the way many of us wake up every morning.

We wake up with no plan, no routine, and nothing scheduled for the day. We fail to plan our day, set a goal, and even worse we have no goals for the week. It's nobody's fault, but yours — for failing to plan what you want to accomplish that day.

DAILY ROUTINE

Let's go back to the morning. Scenario number two: your alarm goes off, you give yourself five seconds to get out of bed, maybe ten, and you tell yourself five things that you're grateful for that morning.

Maybe you even pull out your gratitude journal and you jot down five things that you're grateful for. You might write down: I'm grateful for my health. I'm grateful for my spouse. I'm grateful for my children. I'm grateful that I even have a bed to sleep in.

I strongly encourage everyone reading this chapter to start planning a morning routine. Win the morning and you win the day. It's crucial to the success of one's life to have a morning routine and plan your day to succeed. I highly recommend you train yourself. It's not going to be easy at first.

> WIN THE MORNING AND YOU WIN THE DAY.

It's going to be challenging. It's going to be hard, but the true challenge is going to come three or four weeks down the road when your old habits want to kick in and take over. Remind yourself, you are worth it! You can do this!

As you develop your morning routine, every morning when you open your eyes, get out of bed, spend the first five to ten minutes just being grateful.

Be grateful for everything God has blessed you with. Focus on five things that you are grateful for. After you are done, tell yourself several affirmations out loud.

AFFIRMATIONS

I love myself!

I believe in myself!

I am going to have a great day!

Something great is going to happen today!

I will succeed today!

When you begin your morning with this action, it helps you build positive momentum for your day. You are going to notice you will feel more energized, you will feel more alive. Your heart is going to be in the right place. As you spend three to five minutes telling yourself these affirmations, you will feel empowered. Look into your eyes as you say these powerful words. The eyes of a person is the gateway to their soul. Sometimes your soul needs to hear that you love yourself, that you believe in yourself.

There's no better way to build up your self-confidence and strengthen the inner you than waking up every morning and telling yourself that you love yourself. Your self-confidence or self-esteem is the way you see yourself. You can edify and strengthen your heart and soul by telling yourself these three simple words: I love you. You'll see the transformation if you do this every single day.

Fast forward to the evening. Tell yourself, "I love myself" before you go to bed. It is one of the best things you can do to set up your next day for success. Those words will marinate in your subconscious mind and speak to you.

I WANT YOU TO BEGIN ENVISIONING THE FUTURE LIFE YOU WANT TO LIVE.

After you're done with your five minutes of gratitude, spend around ten minutes meditating. Reflect on the goals you want to accomplish for the day and for the year. Envision yourself completing those goals. Envision yourself buying your new home and acquiring your desired professional position. I want you to begin envisioning the future life you want to live.

As you invest time in the morning envisioning yourself being victorious, throughout the day all the forces of the universe come to you and aid you. Suddenly, everything starts falling into place. You start asking yourself, "How did this happen? It's too good to be true."

That's the power of having a morning routine. All the forces of the universe come to your aid and lift you to a higher standard of living. Once you are done with your ten minutes of meditating, envisioning your future,

PUT IT ON PAPER

I encourage you to write down your goals. If you don't have a goal journal, go and buy one! It will be one of the best investments you will make. Start by writing five goals you have for your personal and professional life. It doesn't have to be a full page of goals, so don't overwhelm yourself.

Simply write all you want to accomplish for the day, and a couple goals you have for the year. One may even be a spiritual goal.

There's a saying, "Goals equal gold." When you write them down and you read them to yourself everyday it speeds up the process of achieving them.

They will shape the future you desire. If you want to know what your life is going to be like five years from now, what books are you reading today? What goals have you set for your future life today? The goals you write down today are going to give you the future you desire tomorrow.

Whatever you focus on you will attract into your life. It's like they put you on the fast track to success. It's like a super highway. Goals position you on an Autobahn highway where there's no speed limit so you reach your destination that much faster. Now that you have successfully written your goals down, put some action into your day.

HEALTH IS WEALTH

Create some momentum in your daily activities. Don't begin your day with eating a big unhealthy breakfast with greasy food and donuts. Develop some healthier eating habits which will give you the energy you will need throughout the day.

Another form of action is daily exercise. It doesn't have to be a marathon run. It doesn't have to be a strenuous four-hour workout. I'm exaggerating these workout regiments, but put some form of physical training into your morning routine. You don't need to be great to start but you do need to start to be great in life.

Begin your morning with a fifteen-minute workout or walk around the block. Some form of exercise is better than nothing. I guarantee you, when you put some form of physical activity into your morning routine, you'll get to work energized and you'll feel like Superman or Wonder Woman!

You'll think more positively. You will feel empowered. You will feel a burst of energy. You will be ready to work, full of life, and full of passion. There isn't anything that could come your way in the morning and derail you from what you desire to accomplish. You will be laser focused.

For many of us, we wake up on the total opposite side of the spectrum. We wake up every morning using the shotgun effect. We start doing random things as soon as we jump out of bed. No organization, no plan, nothing scheduled, and that's why many of us fail to complete or achieve our goals.

Look back at your life and think about some of the chaotic moments you've had. Would situations and circumstances have turned out differently if you would have planned your daily activities, if you had a morning routine?

I encourage you to form these new habits. Organize your day. Start by prioritizing the events you have for the day and for the week. When you begin to strategize your day, it gives you a path to success. Don't just wake up and hope to be successful, have a great day with your family, or to have a great day at work. Be intentional about it! Plan it. Calendarize it. The more you find yourself scheduling events, things you want to accomplish, the more successful you will be.

You are worth it. Invest in your morning every single day. It is vital to the life that you want to live. To live your best life now, you need to develop a morning routine. Remember, just because you've never attempted it before doesn't mean you can't be successful. You are unique. You are capable of accomplishing great achievements in your life. You are powerful beyond your imagination. You are greatness!

YOU HAVE
SO MUCH
ENERGY AND
LIFE INSIDE
OF YOU.

You have so much energy and life inside of you. You haven't even begun to tap into it. As you develop your morning routine of success, don't be the individual that wakes up, rolls on their side, and the first thing they do is look at their social media feed on their cell phone. This is called reaction mode. Instead of being proactive to start your day, you set yourself up to react. The most productive people are proactive.

NO DISTRACTIONS

The best advice I can give you is to start leaving your phone at least fifteen feet away from you at night when you go to bed. Maybe in the bathroom charging because research has proven, if you see your cell phone light up, it hinders your sleeping. Many of us wake up and we wonder why we feel so tired and restless. The reason is we deprive our bodies and minds of the adequate amount of sleep that it requires.

Another major cause of our restlessness is right before we go to bed we are playing with our phones, we are looking at Facebook or playing video games. The last memory our subconscious mind has is the social media feed.

Make it a habit to leave your phone alone thirty minutes prior to going to sleep. When you place your phone next to you, on your nightstand, your chances of receiving the proper sleep your body requires goes down dramatically. The temptation is ever present when we awake in the middle of the night to get a drink of water and lay eyes on our phone to grab it. Don't do it!

That isn't the way to win the morning. It isn't how you're going to win the day. Get in the habit of leaving your phone away from you. Invest those first twenty to thirty minutes of your morning to yourself. Be proactive, not reactive. As you develop these morning habits, you're going to see your life transform in a positive way.

> YOU ARE GOING TO BE A NEWER AND BETTER VERSION OF YOURSELF.

You are going to be a newer and better version of yourself. You are going to love yourself more. You are going to have more confidence in your abilities. You are going to start being aware of more opportunities in your life. It's going to catapult you to new levels of success.

Your morning routine is something that can't be bought. Take time for yourself because when you rush through your morning, you will rush through your day.

ACTION IS THE
FOUNDATIONAL KEY
TO ALL SUCCESS.

— PABLO PICASSO

REFLECTION
CHECK POINT

1. What does your morning routine currently look like?

_____

_____

_____

2. What new habits can you implement to have a more successful day?

_____

_____

_____

3. Do you have daily affirmations? If not, create them TODAY!

_____

_____

_____

CHAPTER 11

POSITIVE DISSATISFACTION

You may be wondering what in the world this could be? Let me tell you, it's the balance between optimism and the need to improve. Too many people today are living mediocre lives. Their lives aren't satisfying their inner being, their true purpose in life. There's such a thing as having a positive dissatisfaction in your life. It's okay to want more in life. It's okay to go out there and make a difference in people's lives.

I dare you to dream big! Why don't you truly make a difference in this world? Not just for your own selfish ambition, but to make mankind better. Are you motivated by a positive dissatisfaction that God wants you to have?

If we do not realize we are blessed in this life, how can we be a blessing to the people around us? However, most of us settle for an average life. We have been trained to settle in life. We have convinced ourselves that our life isn't so bad.

If you've been taught this, I want to challenge you today to birth a new way of thinking. You're not being greedy for having a healthy dissatisfaction. You're not being selfish for wanting better living conditions.

My first full-time job was at a company called Plant Interscapes in San Antonio, Texas. I really loved working there. It was a great organization and it was a great experience to work for Mike Senneff. He was a fantastic leader and always showed his appreciation of me. I consistently wanted to go above and beyond for him.

He always challenged himself and the vision he had. At the time, Plant Interscapes was a good-sized company. They had an office in San Antonio and Austin, which I thought was astonishing. He branched out to Austin during the recession San Antonio had back in the 1980s.

Mike ventured out to develop new business. He didn't allow the economic circumstances to dictate the future of Plant Interscapes. As he acquired new business, the reputation of our organization grew to be known as one of the best interior landscaping companies in Texas.

He established himself as a great leader in my eyes. Most organizations wouldn't have survived. His positive dissatisfaction to thrive, not survive, allowed Plant Interscapes to become the multi-million dollar corporation it is today.

Plant Interscapes always gave back to their employees and continuing education was a huge benefit of working there. They were always sending us to seminars or held conferences for employees to attend. I soon became a manager and wanted to follow in Mike's footsteps. My goal was to influence people in a positive manner the way Mike had influenced me. Leadership is influence.

Interior landscaping does make an office building or hotel come to life with captivating green foliage and decorative ceramic containers. Plain and simple plants add life to a dull setting. Mike enjoyed seeing people receive the benefits plants brought to the work place. It was a positive dissatisfaction to create more jobs in all the major metroplexes in the great state of Texas.

Many leaders become complacent in their organizations. They're satisfied with being an okay business, not taking the leap of faith that Mike did to augment and advance Plant Interscapes. They begin leading with a scarcity mindset and before you know it, they're in the red and wondering how they got there.

On the other hand, the Mikes of the world never settle. They want to be the best in their respected industries in order to serve others. It's difficult to want more for yourself or organization, but you can't get the employees on board.

I learned that it was okay to think outside the box, to challenge your limitations and want more. I learned that having positive dissatisfaction in my life is a delightful thing. I'm not talking about a selfish ambition to want more for yourself. As we advance more as individuals, we have more to offer

> I LEARNED THAT IT WAS OKAY TO THINK OUTSIDE THE BOX, TO CHALLENGE YOUR LIMITATIONS AND WANT MORE.

to the people around us. We can lift them up to a higher level of being.

Fast forward from 20 years to the present, Plant Interscapes is stronger and employing more people than ever. They are well-known and respected throughout the country because they had a leader that carried within himself the positive dissatisfaction to do and be more. I believe Mike exceeded the vision he had as a young leader and business owner.

He has a legacy to build upon and a corporation that's going to continue to impact the marketplace for many years. Mike is a visionary, always pushing his employees to improve all aspects of their lives. I truly respect him for that and I learned so much from him.

How many of us would've risked venturing out of our comfort zones? My guess is that most of us would've been satisfied with producing average or below average results for our business. We would accept the outcome and never questions the possibilities. We would dismiss our convictions of settling and convince ourselves that the situation could be worse.

That's what many small business owners and leaders of organizations probably say. That's the reason why many small businesses and organizations fail and don't profit like they should. They lack the power of positive dissatisfaction. They're content with business as usual, with no desire to expand or step out of their comfort zones.

Now, I don't want you to be greedy. I understand that some people are ambitious for the wrong reasons. Those people have a negative ambition, a selfish ambition. That's not what I'm describing here. What I'm talking about is the positive dissatisfaction to desire more and do more for the people in your community.

I'm not telling you to go out into the world and step on people to get where you want to be. That's not what I'm implying at all. That ambitious, greedy type of success is only temporary. Imagine the difference you could make in people's lives, the positive impact in hiring an extra employee or two.

LIFE OF ABUNDANCE

In all areas of our lives, God wants to give us so much more than we have. God wants to escalate our careers. God wants to supersize our lives! You may only want a Happy Meal life, but God wants to supersize it. The truth is, many of us are sated with living average lives.

I want to embolden you to take a leap of faith and believe He has greater victories in store for your life. Do it for your children and grandchildren. They will thank you for it.

You have so much potential inside of you. You would be astounded at what you could accomplish in your life, career and relationships. For one day, I wish you could see yourself the way God sees you and witness all of the boundless opportunities that are right in front of you. You can have

> YOU HAVE SO MUCH POTENTIAL INSIDE OF YOU.

everything you desire and you have the ability to accomplish anything.

It's okay to have positive dissatisfaction; it's okay to want more out of life. There's nothing wrong with setting a higher standard for you and your children's lives. I've met many people who celebrate other people's successes and that's magnificent. We should be edifying and uplifting each other. The irony is, they don't believe it for themselves.

We celebrate other people's victories. We celebrate their accomplishments, but deep down we can't envision it for ourselves. We feel a sense of guilt if we desire to achieve more in life. It's not your fault. Remember, our reasoning and principles are the result of the environment we were raised in.

The same way God made it happen for others, God wants to make it happen for you. He wants to bless you! He wants you to be successful! He wants you to enlarge the vision you have for your life. Don't walk around imagining you only deserve a cup of blessings. Instead, know that you are worthy of an ocean of blessings. You can't begin to conceive how much God longs to bless you. Seek Him first and watch what happens.

> THE SAME WAY GOD MADE IT HAPPEN FOR OTHERS, GOD WANTS TO MAKE IT HAPPEN FOR YOU.

VISUALIZE THE PRIZE

While attending Robert E. Lee High School my senior year, one of the students walked in carrying a Lexus brochure. She explained that her and her mother stopped by the dealership and picked up a brochure on a particular vehicle she wanted.

At the time, I thought she was crazy. She wanted a Lexus, which is a luxury brand. Those vehicles are expensive. She went on to explain it was the car she was going to purchase in the future. It was her dream car and she was going to attain it. I asked her why she didn't just buy a regular vehicle, a domestic one that's more affordable. She had her heart set on the Lexus.

I now understand that she was envisioning owning her dream car. She was attracting it to herself. She was filled with confidence that she would achieve her goal. She asked me, "Why should I be satisfied with something I don't want, when I can dream big?"

Don't pray and ask for things to be simple and unchallenging in your life. Live with the positive dissatisfaction to be more so that you may do more.

PERMISSION TO SUCCEED

Give yourself the permission to go back to school and finish your degree. Give yourself permission to work harder for the promotion you desire at work. Give yourself permission to go buy the house you've always wanted for your family. Give yourself permission to want more out of life so that you may be a blessing to others.

I want to remind you whose child you are. You are a child of God. He is the Heavenly father that loves you and wants the best for you. If God placed a desire in your heart, He had a reason. It's not an accident. Perhaps, the new car He wants to bless you with is going to help you give someone a ride to work or church. Open your heart and listen to what God is telling you.

Currently, all you depict is a sidewalk of opportunity in front of you. God wants you to think bigger. He wants you to behold a freeway of blessings and opportunities in your life. As a parent, you want the best for your children, don't you? Well, what are you to God? You are His child, and as your parent He desires the best for you.

We serve a God of abundance. We serve a God that is able. We serve a God that is willing. We serve a God that is all-powerful! He didn't create us to get by or barely make it through. He created us to live fulfilled lives.

YOU MUST
REMAIN FOCUSED
ON YOUR JOURNEY
TO GREATNESS.

— LES BROWN

REFLECTION
CHECK POINT

1. What areas are you most satisfied?

_____

_____

_____

2. What ways can you improve your life?

_____

_____

_____

3. What dream do you have for your life?

_____

_____

_____

CHAPTER 12

YOU WERE BORN TO FLY

D id you know you were created for greatness? When God created you, He knew exactly what He was doing. He created a masterpiece. He didn't make a mistake by giving you your skin color. He didn't make a mistake by giving you the wrong hair color. He didn't make a mistake by making you too tall or too short. He knew exactly what he was doing. You are created in the image and likeness of God.

I want you to love yourself exactly the way you are. When you look in the mirror, stare at yourself. You are unique. You are incredible. You are born to fly. You are exactly where you're supposed to be.

You are not here by accident; you have a purpose. God created you with a purpose and your responsibility is to seek that purpose. What drives you? What moves you? What catches your attention? The answers to those questions will help you find your purpose and passion in life.

Too often, we remain in jobs for five, ten, even fifteen years where we are not being fulfilled. We get comfortable and complacent. The reason why you're not happy is because you weren't created to sit in a cubicle for eight to ten hours. Think about this, if you were born to fly, is being in a cubicle all day achieving that goal?

YOU ARE NOT HERE BY ACCIDENT; YOU HAVE A PURPOSE.

Think of the eagle. An eagle soars through the sky, fearless and magnificent.

I would say you need to get out of your comfort zone. The best way to find your purpose in life is to spend some time alone. Seek God and pray for Him to reveal what direction you should take.

When God created you, He equipped you with everything you need to accomplish your purpose in life. He equipped you with everything you need to fly. God already knows the plans He has for you. In Jeremiah 29:11 it says, "For I know the plans I have for you" declares the Lord, "Plans to prosper you and not to harm you, plans to give you hope and a future."

I want to challenge you to spread your wings and soar like the eagle you are meant to be. God already has it all figured out for you. He already knows everything you need to be successful in life and to accomplish the destiny you were created for.

God already has all the right people that are supposed to come into your life and help guide you along your path. He already has all the resources that you need. You might be saying to yourself, I don't have the money that I need, I don't have all the resources that I need. It's not your responsibility. Leave worry, doubt, and fear in God's hands.

> LEAVE WORRY, DOUBT, AND FEAR IN GOD'S HANDS.

STORMS WILL COME

Life will happen unexpectedly. Did you know that an eagle knows when a storm is approaching long before it breaks?

The eagle will fly to some high spot and wait for the winds to come. When the storm hits, it sets its wings so that the wind will pick it up and lift it above the storm. While the storm rages below, the eagle is soaring above it.

The eagle does not escape the storm. It simply uses the storm to lift it higher. It rises on the winds that bring the storm. When the storms of life happen, like the eagle, we can rise above them and ride the winds of the storm that bring sickness, tragedy, failure, and disappointment into our lives. You will never be able to avoid the storms, but you can learn from them and just like the eagle, you can overcome them and not let it prevent you from moving forward in your life.

GOD'S PLAN

If God showed you all the plans He has for you, you would be astonished. The word of God says that eyes have not seen, ears have not heard the plans that He has for you. Expect God's best for your life. Expect God's favor in every aspect of your life. You were born to fly! You were born for greatness.

One of the main reasons we don't accomplish our purpose in life is that we want everything to come easy. We want everything to come to us without a price that we have to pay. People don't realize that when they ask for everything to be easy, they are asking for weakness. If you're not being challenged in life, then you're not growing.

You're not developing into the creation that God meant for you to be. God created so many possibilities within you, but you need to open your heart and mind to see them. You, as a human being, are more powerful than you assume. You are more capable than you think. You are a masterpiece.

> GOD CREATED SO MANY POSSIBILITIES WITHIN YOU, BUT YOU NEED TO OPEN YOUR HEART AND MIND TO SEE THEM.

God doesn't make mistakes, so stop seeing yourself as one. You are beautifully and wonderfully made exactly the way God wanted you. You are the person you are meant to be. I want you to do yourself a favor; every time you look at the person in the mirror, look at the person you will become, not the person you currently are. I don't want you looking at yourself in your current situation. The life you are currently living does not dictate who you are.

I want you to start seeing yourself as the person you are going to become. Remember this, you are not a human being, you are a human becoming. You are becoming everything you were meant to be. You are becoming the champion God created you to be. There is greatness inside of you, your responsibility is to tap into it. It's within you.

When you start realizing you were born to fly, that's when the remarkable happens. You start receiving and attracting things that were meant to be yours from the very beginning. God delights in prospering his children and blessing them abundantly above and beyond our wildest dreams.

He is an amazing father who loves us with all His heart. God doesn't want us going through life struggling. He wants us to live a fulfilled life. He wants us to live a life full of joy and happiness so we may be a blessing to the people around us.

Think about this, if we ourselves are not blessed, how can we be a blessing to other people? The beauty of it all is, since we were born to fly, we were born to be blessed and highly favored by God. Think of yourself as a parent, don't you want the best for your children?

Don't you want the best for your kids and help them achieve mind-blowing things in life? My guess would be that your answer to these questions are a definite yes! In the same way, God being our father and us being his children, He wants us to prosper so we may live a life that impacts and helps transform people into the best version of themselves.

There are hundreds of people out there in the world that God will bring into your life. Your responsibility is to be a blessing to them. Many people are hurting and need assistance, some sense of direction.

They need someone to come into their life and uplift them, encourage them to see that there is hope. When God opens the eyes of your heart and you realize you are a blessing, you will see that it feels good to help other people. You really begin to soar when you give more of yourself because you receive so much more.

Many people out there in the world don't have a sense of direction or purpose. The reality is, they are living their lives on autopilot. They are living life with no joy, no happiness and no true fulfillment in life. They are living their lives as robots without a pulse, just trying to survive.

I am here to tell you, you were not created just to survive. You were not created to barely get by. You were not created to live an ordinary life. God created you to live an extraordinary life.

You are meant to live a life full of passion, full of hope and full of energy. You were created to thrive in this world. What are you waiting for? Go out there and experience the new life God has waiting for you!

He has new beginnings for you today. Live the life you were intended to live. You were born to soar, you were born to create, you were born to be magnificent. My desire for your life is after you finish reading this book, you will become the person God created you to be.

HAVE FAITH NOT FEAR

Is fear keeping you from moving forward? Are you terrified of the unknown? While I have not been skydiving myself, I am going to share a few insights from when Will Smith told the story about his skydiving experience. Of course, everyone has a daily confrontation with fear, but it's how you handle it that matters.

Will Smith begins his story about being in Dubai and him and a few friends had went out one night. One of them had a 'great' idea to maximize the time they had and suggested skydiving. I believe a few drinks may have been involved, so everyone agreed eagerly. He made it to his hotel room and the reality of what he had just committed to hit him!

He said he had the worst night's sleep he ever had — because all he could do was think about what he agreed to do! It didn't become real until he made the commitment with other people. The same people who agreed to the terms. He thought surely they won't follow through with it, but he didn't want to be the one that backed out.

He woke up the next morning after having night sweats for the duration of the night, full of fear and pure terror. Everything in him wanted someone to just speak up and change their mind, but no one did. He made it for breakfast, everyone was there. They get in the van — not one person hesitates. They are all hyping each other up and everyone is moving forward with the plans they made the night before.

They see the airplane. It's almost to the point where they won't be able to back out... he looks around, hoping SOMEONE would say SOMETHING — and NOTHING HAPPENED. They are briefed on safety - and enter the plane.

Secured for take off, they are lifted in the air; 14,000 feet to be exact. He sees a set of lights. Red. Yellow. Green. He processed everything that was going on around him. No one had backed out yet and he refused to be the one to say no. As the light turned green, the door of the plane opened. It was in that moment he realized he had never been on a plane with the door open. Thankfully he made his way to the back so he wasn't one of the first to go.

Once it was his turn, he gets to the edge of the plane and looks down. They tell him they were going to JUMP on 3! He nodded his head in agreement.

1......2...PUSH.....! He wasn't able to JUMP. They are trained to push people on two because most people try to hold onto the plane if they were to say three! He then realized the maximum amount of danger was the minimum amount of fear. He described it as being one of the most exhilarating and phenomenal moments in his life.

But after he thought about it, he realized he was afraid for no reason. How many times are you afraid of something, anticipating the outcome only to realize that there was nothing to be scared of in the first place? Don't spend your time being terrified of something that only exists in your mind! God places the best things in life on the other side of fear.

Have the courage to be a risk taker. You were born to fly with the eagles. You were born for greatness!

SPREAD YOUR WINGS
AND FLY.
YOU WERE BORN
TO SOAR
THROUGH LIFE
WITH MAGNIFICENCE
AND CONFIDENCE.

— TRUDY VESOTSKY

REFLECTION
CHECK POINT

1. What storms are you facing that are keeping you from flying?

_____

_____

_____

2. How have you confronted your fears?

_____

_____

_____

3. In what areas of your life are you soaring?

_____

_____

_____

CONCLUSION

When someone makes the choice to skydive and plummet from a plane, the parachute is equipped with everything they need to land safely. I have shared everything you need to FLY; all you have to do is make the decision to JUMP! We all have the power within us to create the future life we desire. Every day of our lives needs to be committed to growing and developing, becoming a better version of ourselves.

Is there anything that stood out to you? Use it and apply the principles that have been shared to improve the quality of your life. Everyone is in a different stage of life; one chapter might have spoken more to you than others. I encourage you to take action on that chapter and take one step at a time. Focus on small victories daily.

You are capable of living a life filled with happiness, joy, and prosperity, a life full of blessings. It all starts in the morning as soon as you open your eyes. Start everyday with a heart full of gratitude and appreciation. When you focus on the good, you attract more good into your life. Develop a positive mindset that will serve you personally and professionally. Attitude truly is everything.

If you don't expect great things for your life they will never arrive. Expect God's best; expect God's favor everyday of your life. Use your imagination to dream big! Take a drive to go test drive the dream car you have been wanting. Go visit some new model homes and envision you and your family living there. Envision your children playing outside your new home with your dream car in the driveway.

I challenge you to break through limiting beliefs which are holding you back. You were born to succeed in life. You weren't born to be mediocre.

Refuse to go to the grave with so much life still inside of you. Always remember, your best days are in front of you. Your eyes have not seen, nor your ears heard, what God has in store for you.

My contribution to your success in life is this book. *You Were Born to Fly* will guide you down the road toward success. Forgive yourself and forgive others and you will experience the freedom you have been longing for. Next, develop a morning routine that suits your lifestyle. Custom tailor one that you will follow and apply daily. You can do this!

Don't be scared to act on your thoughts and ideas. Don't let the fear of failing keep you from flying.

I want to encourage you to always believe in yourself and in your abilities. Never give up on yourself! You are greatness in the making. I look forward to hearing all the success stories from everyone on how your lives have been enriched. Your destiny is waiting for you. What are you waiting for? Go after it!

"You were born to fly!"

— **Daniel Gomez**